AF444397

Contents

SEVEN SIMPLE WAYS TO MAKE YOURSELF INSTANTLY MORE ATTRACTIVE

You can boost your allure with a few easy body language changes.

Whilst there's only so much you can do to change your looks, there are ways you can instantly increase your attractiveness to others.

Studies show that changes to your body language, your actions and even what you wear can boost your appeal.

So don't overhaul your looks by dying your hair, embarking on a fad diet or getting a spray tan, embrace who you are but make yourself more attractive with these scientifically proven methods.

Here are seven simple things you can do that instantly make you more attractive:

1. Be altruistic

Helping others with no thought for yourself has been shown to be more attractive than good looks when it comes to those looking for a long-term relationship.

A study found that average-looking men who gave money to a homeless person were deemed more attractive to women than better looking men who walked straight past. This wasn't the case for women looking for short-term flings though.

2. Use metaphorical compliments

According to Chinese researchers, women prefer men who use metaphorical language to compliment them.

They claim that compliments like "Your eyes are morning dew" or "Your smile is a naughty goblin" are better received than literal expressions like "Your lips are so sexy." The theory is that using metaphorical language requires more intelligence than more obvious compliments.

3. Look directly at someone and smile

It's no secret that maintaining eye contact is an effective flirting technique, but according to scientific research, it actually makes you seem more attractive too.

To boost your appeal the most, simply look directly at the target of your affections and smile at them.

4. Wear red

Women with muscular physiques now more attractive than thin peers

Donning a frock or T-shirt in the colour of confidence really can make both men and women more attractive to the opposite sex, research has found.

Wearing red makes men seem more dominant and successful, and when women wear red, they tap into men's primitive desires and thus seem more sexually desirable.

However when we put this theory to the test we had mixed results.

5. Modify your walk

Swaying your hips or adopting a swagger when you walk can make women and men more attractive respectively, according to research.

In fact, you could double your allure simply by walking in a different way. For women, it's a case of swinging your hips from side to side, whereas men should walk with swagger in their shoulders.

6. Nod your head

People appear up to 40 per cent more attractive to others simply by nodding their head.

In fact, a study found that doing so makes someone seem more approachable and likeable, and thus more attractive.

7. Adopt an expansive posture

Whether in a picture on your dating app profile or just the way you look across the bar, adopting an expansive posture can make someone seem more attractive, a study found.

This means having your arms and legs facing outwards rather than crossing or folding them - the idea is that expansive postures signal openness and dominance, which are often seen as attractive.

16 Powerful Ways To Attract Men

How to attract a man that you like and how to attract men in general is such a big topic that I get asked about constantly by women.

Have you ever seen or heard of a situation where a woman who isn't particularly gorgeous or "seductive" somehow has men chasing her and constantly trying to hit on her?

I am sure you have come across a woman like this, who somehow effortlessly has men wildly attracted to her. And not just any men...

What is it that "those kind" of women are doing that makes them so irresistible? Well, in this article I will take you through some of the most common and universally applicable things you can do to make yourself more attractive to men and attract the man you want.

I'm giving you this information all from a man's perspective and I am warning you now… first of all, these are all my opinions at the end of the day.

I am well aware that there are always exceptions and different people like different things. But what I am going to take you through is some of the most common and universally true things that make a man feel attracted to you.

You might or might not be surprised to know that a lot of has to do with your internal mental state. Your internal mental state is what comes across as your "vibe" and overall "persona" that you give off to men. When you are in a bad mood, for example, even if you pretend not to be, it comes across to him.

This leads me to the first mindset that you need to know to attract men.

How Your Mindset Will Attract The Men You Want

1. Manage Your Mood

Making your mood a priority is going to be a huge win for you when it comes to being more attractive.

Why?

Men are instinctively attracted to happy women. When you are in a good mood, he feels this pleasant vibe when he is around you.

Men can sense your vibe and you don't have to say anything to make it come across; in fact, the less you "try" to "prove" what a good mood you are in and the more you focus on actually being in a good mood, the better off you will be.

2. Have Fun

Do things you enjoy. Take the time out to do fun things in your life where you can let loose and really laugh and have fun with things.

Whether it's going out with friends and having a good time or spending time with family and living life in a happy, fun way. Experience life in the moment and don't dwell on trivial things that don't matter.

If you genuinely have fun and are happy, this automatically makes you more attractive to men. Men are attracted to happy women who can laugh a lot and are happy. Don't fake it; this comes off as fake and won't be attractive.

3. Don't Compare Yourself To Other Women

I understand the instinct to compare yourself to other women and to other people in general. Maybe you see another woman and you think to yourself, "if only I had ...." (insert whatever it is that you wish you could change about yourself that she has).

Take this mindset and put it aside.

The reason I am saying to you this is because when you compare yourself, all you do is make yourself feel miserable and frustrated. The best thing to do is be your best self and focus on things you can control and improve upon. This will make you feel good.

4. Do What Feels Comfortable

You might have heard that wearing a wacky outfit, getting a strange sex toy contraption or doing some super sensual and risqué is the only way to attract a man.

Forget all of this. Trying to "do things" that you are completely uncomfortable with because you think it will attract a man is a horrible idea because you will not be comfortable.

Being comfortable is essential when it comes to being attractive to a man. If you are comfortable, you will find that everything you do is naturally and effortlessly more attractive to men.

So don't think that you have to do anything that makes you feel awkward and unnatural because it won't help you anyway.

5. Know Yourself

Self-discovery is an ongoing process that we all go through in our lives. We are always growing and changing as people.

This is an important step when it comes to being attractive: get to know yourself as much as you can and this will automatically make you feel more confident and comfortable.

What I mean by know yourself is know your strengths and weaknesses and be able to identify what you are good at and what you aren't naturally good at.

These mindsets are going to automatically make you more attractive to men.

How Your Appearance Will Attract The Men You Want

Obviously physical appearance is a topic that has to be addressed when it comes to making a man attracted to you.

It's a fact of life: men and human beings are visual creatures. There are certain things a man is going to respond to whether he wants to or not. I'm only giving you this information to help you... not to offend or be rude, so please

6. Makeup

Every man has different preferences when it comes to makeup, but there is a consistent theme with what most men seem to find attractive.

For me personally, I like it when a woman puts in effort to do makeup that enhances how she already looks but does not pile on the foundation and then add a bunch of different powders and whatnot to it.

I have seen women wearing those huge fake eyelashes for example and then a ton of fake tanner on and so much makeup it was obvious from a mile away… and I suppose some men do find this hot but most would prefer a little bit less.

With that said, a good application of makeup can certainly transform a woman's look so definitely don't be afraid to put on makeup.

7. Fitness/Diet

This is a very sensitive topic and I don't want anyone to get offended and say that I am trying to say all women have to be skinny.

This is not true at all. All I am saying is that being as fit as you possibly can and making healthy eating choices (healthy eating choices not starving) is the key to looking your best.

Listen to your body don't try to look how you naturally can't look without having to starve or be unhealthy. This is key. Healthy is hot.

8. Clothing

Clothing can make a big difference when it comes to being attractive to men. Now, the main thing is that you wear clothes that fit your body well and accentuate your best assets.

Now I am not saying to go out in stripper heels and a nonexistent dress that shows almost your entire body. Unless this is what you like and it makes you feel good, but don't do that because you think it's going to make men more attracted to you.

To be honest, being too skimpy to a point of absurdity when you first meet a man actually might be a turn-off to some men.

The ideal way to dress is a combination of sexy and leaving something to the imagination. But most importantly find clothing that fits your body well and makes you feel good.

9. Hair

Every man has different preferences when it comes to hair and in general all you really need to focus on is that you feel good about it.

Whether it's a simple, layered medium length cut or long hair or shorter hair… The point is that you feel good and make an effort when it comes to doing your hair.

10. Smell

Perfume is actually something that a lot of women over do. Most men do not like very strong perfume. You're better off sticking with something very light and being very conservative with how much you spray.

Being clean is obviously important and goes without saying in terms of smelling good; drenching yourself in perfume is not. One thing most men agree upon is that women's hair normally smells amazing from all the shampoo products and stuff. The point is less is more.

11. Hair "Down There"

Now this is a very individual preference type of situation. You really only need to focus on taking care of this part of your body in terms of hair and do something.

Unless you are going to keep all your hair (rarer these days but again this is a total individual preference and there are some guys who do like this so if there's a man who you know likes this go for it). I would say in general, though, trimming at the very least is a good idea.

There's a lot of debate about being completely bare or being mostly bare and having a landing strip. You can do a bunch of different fun things with this. And another benefit (in addition to men finding it hot) is that YOU will feel sexy knowing you are "groomed" down there. It's just as much for you to feel sexy as it is for him to find you sexy.

Some Really Blunt (And Explicit) Tips To Attract The Men You Want

These are going to be extremely honest and uncensored… but are designed to give you the raw truth and to help you out as much as possible.

The key to most of these is that you are comfortable. If you are not comfortable then there is no point in doing any of these things. If you are, though, it will come off as extremely sexy. Being comfortable is sexy.

12. Touch Yourself in Front of Him and Let Him Watch

It would be extremely difficult to find a man who does not find this to be an insane turn on. I won't really go into this further but I think what I said speaks for itself. Do it in the way that feels comfortable for you and only if it feels comfortable.

13. Be a Lady in the Streets and a "Freak" In the Sheets

Yes. I actually just wrote this cliché. I can't believe I am even writing it but it's such a concise way to describe one of the most attractive things to most men: a woman who is presentable and one way when she's interacting with the world but behind closed doors brings out an entirely different wild, sexual side.

Being able to truly let go in the bedroom is going to make it so much more fun for both you and him. Holding back out of fear of being judged and being awkward will only do a disservice to both you and him.

I realize this may not be comfortable for you, but if you take baby steps and find a way to get truly comfortable "letting go" you will notice how much this turns a man on. Do what feels natural, not what you think you are "supposed to do."

14. Make Your Pleasure A Priority Too

This is important. Some people only care about their own pleasure and others only care about the other person's pleasure.

What's the most attractive way to focus on pleasure? Focus on both your pleasure and his. Make your own pleasure a priority without ignoring the fact that you want him to feel satisfied at the same time.

Ignoring your pleasure is going to do you a disservice because not only will you be missing out on an insane amount of good feelings, but you will lose the opportunity to turn him on!!!

Most men are turned on when they can make a woman feel genuine pleasure. And do not fake it because most men can tell.

15. Tease Him

This one is a bit tricky because there is a fine line between "good" teasing that drives a man crazy in a good way and "bad" teasing that makes a man frustrated and annoyed.

If you are into him and feel sexually attracted to him, let the attraction build up by touching him gently throughout your interactions with him.

Start with innocent touches and be very nonchalant and natural when you do it. For example, if you are sitting next to each other, you could kind of inch a tiny bit closer to him and have your leg against his leg and don't say a word about it, just enjoy the moment. Or you could casually touch his thigh, as if it's the most normal thing in the world.

16. Don't Be Afraid To Be Yourself

When it comes to being attractive to men, all women are different in terms of what makes them uniquely attractive.

Some women are more innocent and cutesy, others more seductive and intense, others a combination of all these... some are more outgoing and expressive, others are more shy and want a man to take control.

Some women are completely unafraid to take control and others like to be dominated. The point is to find what you feel comfortable with and realize that some men will be extremely attracted to you and these particular aspects of your personality.

There is no use trying to be different than how you naturally are, because this is what men find most attractive: a woman who is being genuine and true to herself, her desires and her instincts.

So there you have it. Here is how to attract and be attractive to a man. I hope it helps.

Now that you know more about how to attract the man you want, do you know what you're going to do next? Before you decide you need to know about the pivotal moment in any relationship that determines if you get to live happily ever after or he leaves you so pay attention to this next step because it's vitally important: At some point he will ask himself is this the woman I should commit to for the long term? The answer to that will determine the fate of your relationship: Do you know how men determine if a woman is girlfriend material (the type of woman he commits himself to) or if he see's you as just a fling?

The second problem will undermine whatever relationship you have if it's allowed to fester and destroy your relationship from the inside, so read this right now or risk your relationship because at some point he starts to lose interest. He doesn't call you back or he becomes emotionally closed off. He seems like he's losing interest or pulling away – do you know what to do? If not you're putting your relationship and the future of your love life in great danger, read this now or risk losing him forever:

In summary...

How To Attract The Men You Want

1. Manage your mood

2. Have fun

3. Don't compare yourself to other women

4. Do what feels comfortable

5. Know yourself

6. Makeup

7. Fitness/Diet

8. Clothing

9. Hair

10. Smell

11. Hair "down there"

12. Touch yourself in front of him and let him watch

13. Be a lady in the streets and a "freak" in the sheets

14. Make your pleasure a priority too

15. Tease him

16. Don't be afraid to be yourself

13 Things A Woman Can Do To Be More Attractive To Men

I have read my share of Thought Catalog in the past few months, and it seems like men have really tiptoed around the subject of holding women to some kind of a standard. Well, I'm going to ignore that paradigm and speak on what I think men look for in a woman. So, here is yet another listicle for our wonderful readership.

1. Stay in Shape

We want to be aroused by the sight of you being naked. People can argue the pitfalls of the BMI scale all they want, but for the average Jane, it works just fine. Men don't want a bag of bones, nor do they want a woman who looks like she is smuggling beach balls. I suggest 3-

4 times a week of cardio-esque activity. Regarding your diet…you do not need to starve yourself; you do not need those greasy chips either.

2. Lay Off the Body Modification

Men gravitate to natural hair color, tasteful and coverable tattoos (if any at all), and piercings that are not out of control and all over the place.

3. Make Your Own Money

When it comes to money, men really couldn't care less if you make a whole lot, but you need to be making enough so that you are not a financial drain on him. If you make more than him, more power to you, just refrain from throwing it in his face like some form of one-upmanship.

4. Be Feminine

Men want to date WOMEN, not men with vaginas.

5. Be Submissive

This kind of overlaps with being feminine. As much as the word has been made into a negative, being submissive is a good thing, and it's not synonymous with being a door mat or that you have no voice in the relationship. Seriously, heaven forbid you do a little back bending for the sake of pleasing YOUR man because you want to keep him interested in you. Personally I think feminism has turned relationships that are supposed to be loving into their own little battlefields. Rub his back, watch what he wants to watch, suck him off. A GOOD man will reciprocate, and placate to the things you want and make sure you are also happy.

6. Sex Life

Men want a woman that has a healthy sex drive and few past sexual partners. That means that you and your past boyfriend had a lot of sex. It does not mean that you were the town bicycle. We get it, you want to be able to sleep with the college football team and not be judged for it the same way he ran through the cheerleading squad (insert "Master Key/Shitty Lock" analogy). Life isn't fair. Get used to it. The average Joe will never see that many women anyway. Men also do not want a woman that leverages sex as a way to get what she wants. That is a pretty good indicator that she really is not all that interested in sex [with him] in the first place.

7. Be Intelligent

No man wants a woman that cannot flex her mental muscles.

8. Be Childfree

This is kind of the not-so-secret secret. Men don't want instant families, nor do they want the ultimate form of cuckoldry that is raising another man's child. This goes double if you have multiple children and/or if your children are biracial. It does not matter if your child's father was abusive, a deadbeat, a good man, or hit by a bus tragically. The bottom line is that you have a child, and it does not belong to the eligible bachelors out there.

Fun fact: In many states, if your child starts to view him as a father figure and you two eventually break up, you can sue him for child support. No, he does not have to

tells women that they are ugly. What is even worse is that half of you come out of the house looking like Bozo the Clown. Maybe you should throw away the Maybelline, and work with what you were born with.

12. Stop Cussing

Coming from someone who is a United States Sailor, it really is not attractive to have a girlfriend that cusses like one. If you think you are such a fucking lady, you had damn well better act like it for once.

13. Stop Hoarding Guy Friends

9 out of 10 of your guy friends just want to sleep with you anyway. Men know how other men think. The first guy that comes to comfort you after a big fight will also be the first one to say "he's not good enough for you" in order to sabotage the relationship, and then he'll be the

first one to try to get into your pants after he convinces

you that your man is a creep. It's not about having trust

issues. It's about knowing how people act. Trust is

earned, not immediately granted.

6 Pre-Emptive Answering To Counterargument Sound Bites:

A. "You don't speak for every man out there." These attributes operate on a bell curve, and more men sit underneath the curve than amongst the outliers. Obviously not every man wants every single trait on here, but the less that you deviate from the standard the more "marketable" you are.

B."That goes both ways." Nice observation. You are fully at liberty to have the same standard(s) for the men you date. You should write an article about it.

C. "Don't tell me what to do or how to be." You can take all of this with a grain of salt for all I care. I am just giving you some insight into the minds of men once the filter has been taken off.

D. "My boyfriend loves me just the way I am." "I don't have XYZ, and I have lot of men chasing after me." Good for you. Everybody settles in some aspect. Holding out for the partner that is perfect in every way is a fool's errand. He has simply learned to accept your faults. Stop deluding yourself. The thirst is strong these days. A saying I heard less than a week ago was, "If you have standards, you're just cock-blocking yourself." Some men will take whatever they can get.

E. "[Insert random hostile comment that attacks me directly.]" Ad hominem. Debate the ideas presented. You will be more productive that way.

F. "I would do this, but...." You can rationalize it all you want. It still doesn't detract from what men want. You can't argue someone into finding you attractive.

How To Impress Your Husband: 12 Tricks To Attract Him All Again

He comes closer to you. Gives a naughty look, and then pulling you nearer to his masculine body, makes you feel wanted. Slowly he starts kissing your neck and just when you get into the mood, you hear the doorbell ring.

Then you wake up, realizing that it was a dream. Of late, such things have been happening just in dreams as you and your partner are busy with work and children. Your sex life takes a back seat.

If your soul mate is becoming more of a roommate and you want it to change, then this article is for you. MomJunction tells you how to turn up the heat, reach your 'sexpectation' and most importantly how to impress your husband.

Types Of Intimacy:

Before we go into the details, let us explain the kind of chemistry every couple should achieve. There are four types of chemistry, and to impress your husband and get the spark back in your life, you need to have them all:

1. Physical chemistry: it generates physical desire and arousal

2. Emotional chemistry: this creates care, affection and trust

3. Mental chemistry: generates interest, compatibility and receptivity

4. Spiritual chemistry: brings respect, appreciation, happiness

12 Simple Ways To Impress Your Husband:

Surely marriages are made in heaven but you have to put some extra effort here on earth to keep it going.

1. Show the gorgeous side of you:

Maintain basic hygiene, comb your hair, smell nice and wear fitted clothes. Dressing well will always have a positive impact. Wear a dress that your husband likes, and brush up your appearance. Wearing clothes that compliment your figure not only make you attractive but also boost your self-confidence.

Get regular haircuts, go for pedicure and manicure, get your arms and legs waxed and have a facial done. Spend some money on good perfume.

2. Update your knowledge:

Men like women who are well-read. They prefer women who know what is happening in the world. An intellectual wife, who can hold a discussion and have her view point on various topics, will keep her husband engaged in a healthy conversation. Read the news paper and novels for starters.

3. Be independent:

Do not depend on him, be it financially or otherwise. A strong independent woman is surely attractive. When it comes to money, men really do not care how much you earn, but they do not want you to be a financial drain on them (well most men).

For your daily tasks as well, avoid seeking help for him. Do your jobs yourself, so he gets tempted to help you.

4. Take care of your health:

Follow a fitness regime. Exercise strengthens your immune system, improves stamina and your concentration. It has added advantage too: it will keep your man attentive and attracted towards you. Seems worth it!

5. Wear your apron for your man:

The way to a man's heart is through his stomach. Cooking is an admirable quality. Your husband will feel special when you cook him his favorite meal. You need not be a great cook, but the fact that you made an effort to cook something, especially for him, matters. Also, cooking together is an awesome way to rekindle your bond. It is an affair with food.

6. Take interest in his interest:

Be it sports, cars, bikes or movies, show interest in what your man likes. He will definitely appreciate the effort you are putting. It will make him feel close to you and this is a great way to spend some quality time together.

7. Express your love:

Show your love, every single day. Let him know how much you value him. Tell him how much you love him. Do something sweet or different for him, for example write 'I love you' on the bathroom mirror for him or slip a small note with his lunch, bake his favorite cake. Care for him in sickness and health.

8. Plan a date night:

Book a table for two in a fancy restaurant or plan it at home. Make your children sleep early. Spend time together, just the two of you.

If you thought that we are giving you just some platonic ideas, no, we are, actually, preparing you for the more physical (read: bolder) ones:

9. Take the initiative:

You need not wait for your man to make the first moves in the bedroom. Let him know you need him, show him you are waiting for these private moments to come. Move your fingers over him seductively, while you keep open your dress just enough to tantalize him. You will surely love what follows next.

10. Give him a surprise:

Surprise him with a naughty encounter whenever you get a chance. Do something mischievous when he is in the bathroom, or in the kitchen or when he is engrossed in his phone.

When the kids are asleep or are not around, wear a sexy dress that you have bought without his knowledge, arouse him with your acts. This will leave him asking for more.

11. A warm bath can do wonders:

Get into a shower with him. Seek his help to undress you, and turn on the shower. Make the bath playful by rubbing his back, while he caresses you. You can make it more seductive by putting some aromatic room freshener or flowers in the bathroom.

12. Get a bit oily:

What can be a better way to relax your husband after a tiring day? Pour aromatic oil on his back, and begin massaging him. Press his shoulders, so that he forgets everything about work and starts thinking about the task ahead.

Being touchy makes things interesting between you and your husband. You need not have to wait for a time and place. Simply steal a moment. And if you do it the right way, a simple gesture like a kiss on his ear can be followed by a long story.

A Right Touch To Turn Him On:

Know how to touch him. There are many places where men would like to be touched to get into the mood:

• Ear: Kiss him behind his ear or whisper sweet nothings into his ear. Use your tongue a little too. Biting the top of the ear lobe lightly or breathing deep behind his ear will drive him crazy.

• Neck: Give pecks on the front or back of your man's neck. Nibble on the nape of his neck. Neck is a very sensitive area, it has several nerve endings and that does the trick.

• Back: Give him a sensual back and shoulder massage. Doing this will increase his blood circulation and relax him. Kiss his back in between the massage session.

• Back of his head: Caress the back of his head while kissing him softly.

• Chest: Stoke his chest gently. Play with his chest hair.

• Butt: Arouse him with a light smack on it. Or massage his butt after you are done with his shoulders and back.

• Foot: A foot massage will relax him and kissing the foot or biting the toe will arouse him.

• Inner thigh: While your husband's sex organ is obviously the most erogenous place of his body, explore the area around to maximize the pleasure.

You need to be confident and bold enough to make the

first move and impress him with your sexuality. And for

that you have to take care of your attractiveness.

How To Be Attractive For Your Husband:

Here's how to attract husband:

1. Get your beauty sleep: No matter how much make-up you wear, you cannot look attractive unless you have enough sleep. A tired face or red eyes do not look appealing. Therefore, sleep for eight hours every day.

2. Smile: When you smile you send signals that you are friendly and approachable and are in a good mood. Smiling is appealing and attractive.

3. Be polite: Talk to him softly, and answer him politely. This will make sure the mood at home is calm. Do not pounce on him if he forgets to switch off the light in the bathroom or leaves his wet towel on the bed.

4. Stand tall: By standing or walking tall, you begin to feel confident and comfortable. This will show on your

face and confident woman attract men. So, keep your head up, and body straight.

5. Maintain eye contact: Look into your husband's eyes when you are talking with him. That makes him understand that you are listening to him and are interested in the conversation.

6. Be feminine: Men like taking care of their girls. They want to feel needed. Show them your delicate side time to time or be a little submissive. Men want to be with women, who look up to them for advice and help.

7. Chill out: Give your man some space. Do not pester your husband about where he is or with whom. Do not nag him if he is on the phone or watching his favorite match on the TV.

Ways To Be Sexy In Bed:

If you expect to have great sex, then you need to work hard for your 'sexpectations'.

1. Splurge a bit on fancy lingerie: Wearing bright red lacy bra or sexy corset will make you the seductress you husband would want. Wear things that suit your body type. Accentuate your assets. Lift the parts that sag.

2. Wear his clothes: There is nothing sexier for a man to see his beautiful wife wearing his clothes. Wear a sexy lingerie with a loose, oversized shirt of your husband and leave the buttons open. Casually do your chores without making it look too obvious.

3. Talk dirty: Tell him what you want him to do to you in bed. Use your finger to write imaginary words on your husband's body. Drive him crazy by whispering sweet nothings into his ear.

4. Lather on oil: Essential oil makes your skin look smoother, shiny and smell good. And that's sexy for a man.

5. Set the stage: Bring on the mood by creating an intimate setting with nice music and dim lights or scented candles. You can also fill the bathtub with warm water and sensuous bath salts, a few rose petals and two glasses of wine. Waiting for him in the tub will be all the more sexy.

6. Add flirtation and seduction to your romance: Men like it. They find it mysterious and exciting, even if you have been married to your man for years.

7. Have some foreplay: Sometimes foreplay is more enjoyable than the sex. The anticipation of what's going to happen next will make your husband want you more.

8. Strip for him: Perform a striptease for your lovely husband. Focus on removing one cloth at a time. Maintain an eye contact. Show him some of your dance moves.

9. Lie down on the bed and cover yourself only with a sheet: Spread your hair across the pillow and cross your arms under your breasts so that you can push them up. Leave top of your cleavage exposed. Show only one leg till calf. A bit of skin showing with rest left for imagination will drive your husband wild!

10. Take initiative: Want to know how to attract husband? Then, get a little bossy in bed. Tell him what you want and what turns you on. You control the moment, men crave for it.

11. Tie him up: And if you want to know how to attract husband in bed, here's an idea. Take control! Some men get excited by the idea of a sexy woman taking control of the situation. Use some comfortable and soft scarf or his tie and tie him to the bed or sofa. Put a comfortable cushion or pillow below his head.

12. Watch porn together: Yes, watching porn together in the bed would make your husband want you more. Giving your husband a visual treat will drive him crazy, and the added advantage is you can mimic those moves.

13. Go slow: Sex is not a fast food. There is no way you can feel satisfied with a quickie. You need to enjoy what you are doing.

The most important thing to remember is that you need not shy away from your husband or feel guilty for having sexual desires. It is not sleazy or vulgar to impress him sexually. It strengthens your bond and makes sure that the physical needs of both you and your husband are met amply.